D1718166

AARHUS CITY HALL

© The Danish Architectural Press, 1991
Printed by: Bogtrykkeriet, Skive
Reproduction: F. Hendriksen's Eftf.
Type: The original type from the City Hall's sign album and Futura Book medium
Translated by Martha Gaber Abrahamsen
Photographs: Jens Lindhe
Graphic design: Jens Lindhe

ISBN: 87 7407 1106

Older black and white photographs in the book were lent by Billedtjenesten, Aarhuus Stiftstidende, and Hammerschmidt Reklame.
The book on Aarhus City Hall was published with financial support from Direktør E. Danielsen og Hustrus Fond, Danmarks Nationalbank's Anniversary Foundation of 1968, and Jørgen Esmers Mindelegat.

CONTENTS

Foreword	6
The Architectural Competition	9
Winning Entries	12
The Revised Design	16
The Design Office in Aarhus	20
Laying the Cornerstone and the Inauguration	24
Aarhus City Hall: Constructions, materials, and artistic decoration by Erik Møller	35
The City Hall's Architecture: The Draped Structure by Kjeld Vindum	77

Photos by Jens Lindhe

AARHUS CITY HALL

"The Aarhus City Council hereby invites Danish architects to take part in a design competition for a new city hall in Aarhus." This was the introduction to the program for an architectural competition published on April 28, 1937.

Fifty-three entries were submitted to the competition on August 2, 1937, and the result of the judging was made public on the morning of Saturday, August 14th. The entry designed by Arne Jacobsen and Erik Møller won first prize.

In 1890, Martin Nyrop had won first prize in the competition for Copenhagen's City Hall, and since then, Danish architects had not vied for such a large public building commission.

Aarhus City Hall was inaugurated on July 2, 1941. This book about the City Hall was published on the occasion of the inauguration's fiftieth anniversary.

ERIK MØLLER

Competition design, August 1937, first prize. Arne Jacobsen and Erik Møller
Opposite: Professor Thomsen presenting the results of the competition

THE ARCHITECTURAL COMPETITION

The designs were to be judged by a committee of architects and City Council members. The architects were Professor Edward Thomsen, chairman, M.K. Michaelsen, and A. Eriksen. The Aarhus City Council appointed Mayor H.P. Christen, and City Council members Stecker-Christensen, J.C. Sørensen, C. Mousten, and J.R. Fænger.
The City Council members later served as the building committee, with the Mayor as chairman.

The expert jury members' recommendation: "The building, with a relatively small ground area and volume, is placed in such a way that a sizable amount of the park remains intact. A number of the old trees are preserved and create the core of an attractive design for a new City Hall park with good access to the streets. Access to the City Hall's two entrances: The main entrance on Sønder Allé and the entrance on Park Allé are well located, the former with a ramp which in itself is lovely, but is not completely appropriate for traffic to and from the building, the latter with a useful parking place in front for visitors to and employees of the City Hall.
"The building's main composition, with the large, deep block around the Main Hall on Sønder Allé and the long, higher office wing on Park Allé, ending with a lower wing on the new street, is attractive and makes it among other things possible in a natural way to satisfy the program's requirement of divisions with fire walls. The layout of the plan is simple, with good vestibules and access to the various institutions. The City Council Chamber is beautifully accentuated, with its projection over the main entrance a dominant element in the facade on Sønder Allé. The Mayor's offices are especially well located in relation to one another and also in relation to the City Council Chamber and adjacent rooms. The Main Hall's great height and the reduced floorspace in relation to it caused by the vestibule's encroachment would be less than optimal acoustically. The staircase in the panoptic corridor is too steep. The restaurant's location is good, but it has no link by stairs with the kitchen facilities in the basement; these facilities, lack direct access to the outside.

"The entry presents a good design for the reinforced concrete construction and an appropriate layout for the building's heating and ventilating systems. More effective ventilation for the City Council's committee and conference rooms is desirable, and the ordinary office facilities should have an air extraction system with fans. The building's exterior has a beautiful, monumental, and festive character which expresses its function in a natural way. The entry's design is exceptionally talented and is an attractive and dignified solution to the assignment presented."
From the description of the competition design: "The Main Hall is given light from the large window in the end wall, which faces directly on the Allé so that this main room in the building provides a beautiful view of a row of trees which subdue the light from the window in a pleasant way."

The Main Hall

From the description of the competition design:
"The Main Hall is given light form the large window in the end wall, which faces directly on the Allé, so that this main room in the building provides a beautiful view of a row of trees which subdue the light from the window in a pleasant way."

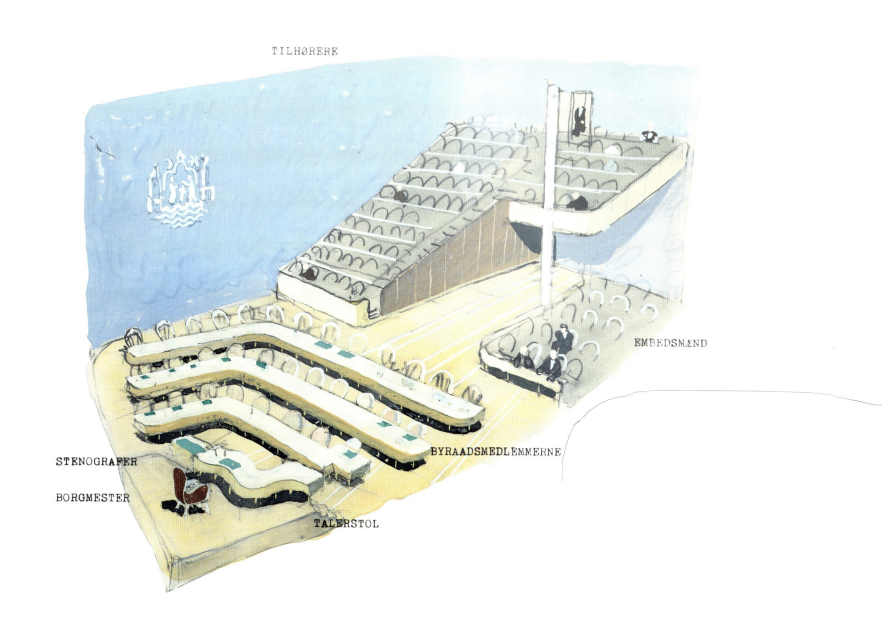

The City Council Chamber

WINNING ENTRIES

Statement by the expert members of the jury:
"Many interesting designs were submitted to the competition which show that the competitors put in a considerable amount of work and which give a comprehensive view of the commission's potentials with a view to placement and design. Several entries do, however, show a lack of respect for, or perhaps knowledge of, the site's fine park-like character which, since the building is intended for this site, provides excellent material with which to create a harmonious entity of great esthetic value in conjunction with the new City Hall.
"In the evaluation of the entries submitted, emphasis has thus been largely placed on the beautiful, appropriate location of the building, and on keeping the volume of the building within reasonable bounds."

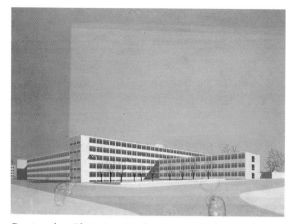

Design by Christian Holst, Aage Holst, and Palle Jacobsen

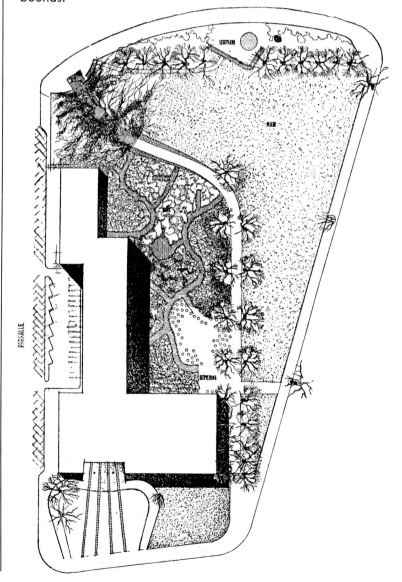

1st PRIZE, Arne Jacobsen and Erik Møller

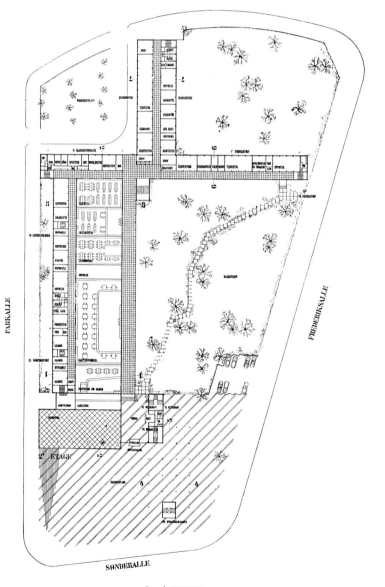

2nd PRIZE

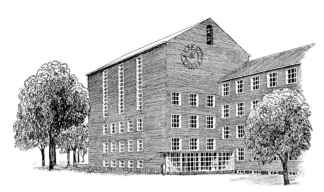

Design by Thomas Havning

Design by H.E. Langkilde and Ib Martin Jensen

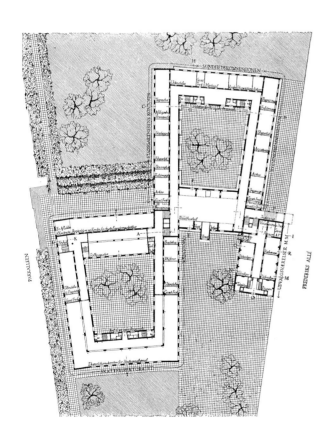

3rd PRIZE

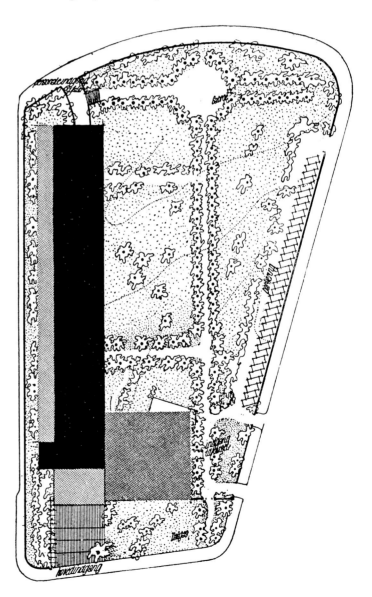

4th PRIZE

Design by Ove Boldt and Knud Dam

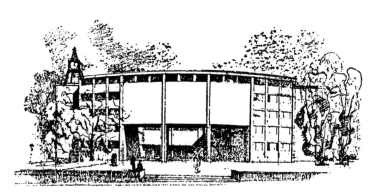

Design by Frits Schlegel and Henning Karlby

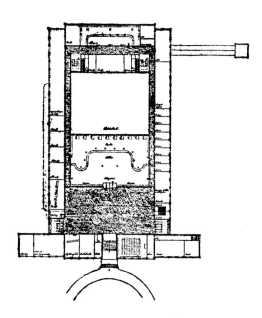

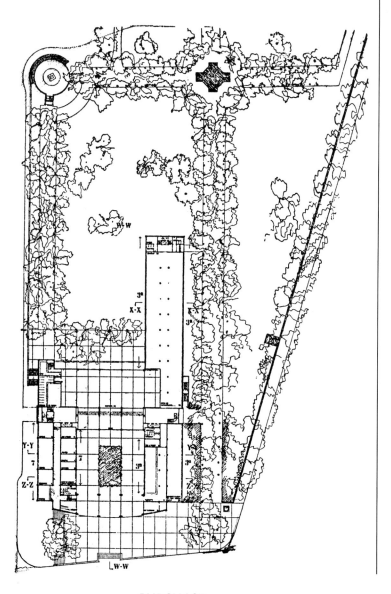

PURCHASE

PURCHASE

Design by N.C. Skjøth

Design by Mogens Lassen and Erhard Lorenz

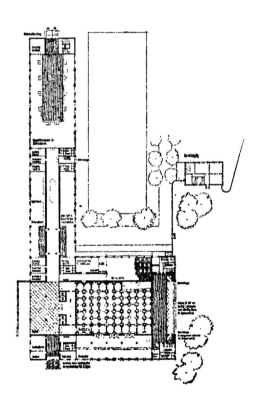

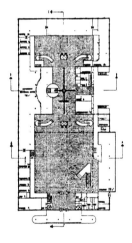

PURCHASE

PURCHASE

THE REVISED DESIGN

The winning entry was given a fine reception in all the daily papers, but there was soon a disappointed outcry, stirred up considerably by the papers.

Opinions were voiced, and such new phrases as "earth-born bricks" and "genuine Jutland dirt" were coined.
When tempers had cooled down, the City Council called in the architects to hear if it was possible to take into account the desire for a more monumental design for the City Hall.

Arne Jacobsen and I went home and reconsidered the matter. The idea of a tower was, after all, a new challenge, and it ended with our proposal for a tower and stone-faced facades.

Politiken, August 23, 1937

We arrived in Aarhus on November 2, 1937, and were immediately received by the City Council, where a heated discussion ensued. Among other things, one of the members of the City Council expressed his pleasure at the "scaffolding around the tower," which symbolized that it had not been completed before it had been given its spire.

The revised design and the final building retained all the main features of our original proposal, but the main entrance with the driveway and the design of the building on Banegårdspladsen with its sixty-meter-high tower with bell, clock, and viewing platform, together with the marble facing, gave the building a more dignified appearance.

Page 15: Revised design, November 1937

Pages 16–17: Facade on Park Allé

Erik Møller, design office at 19 Spanien

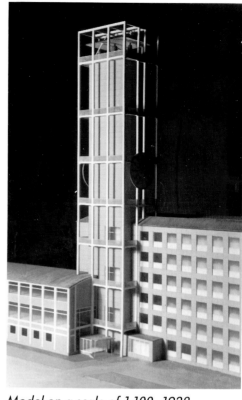
Model on a scale of 1:100, 1938

Luc Regeur and Peder Hagen, design office at 19 Spanien

THE DESIGN OFFICE IN AARHUS

Erik Møller and Arne Jacobsen on the site

The shed on Rådhuspladsen, 1938

We immediately started work on the final drawings and built up a design office especially for the City Hall.

In March 1938 we moved to Aarhus. The design office was housed at 19 Spanien, where the utility company's office building had space available. The architects Per Hagen and Luc Regeur moved with us to Aarhus, and Hans J. Wegner followed later. Everyone settled down nicely and Hagen, Regeur, and I built houses in Aarhus.

There were two resident architects, J.K. Schmidt and C. Ottosen.

The engineering firm of Nieport & Wied, with H.V. Geer as the resident engineer, was responsible for the installations, while the firm of Steensen and Varming, represented by Poul Demant, was responsible for the actual constructions.

After executing the approved design on a scale of 1:200, we made a detailed model on a scale of 1:100. The model was presented to the budget committee.

The first thing to be built on the site was a shed, where the resident architects and engineer had their offices and various meetings were held.

During the German occupation, a number of young architects had joined together and formed the "study circle in Aarhus" with the purpose of graduating from the School of Architecture in Copenhagen. Professor Thomsen provided instruction and C.F. Møller and I were his assistants. The shed was used by the study circle after working hours, and its final project was completed there. The shed thus became a little forerunner of the School of Architecture in Aarhus.

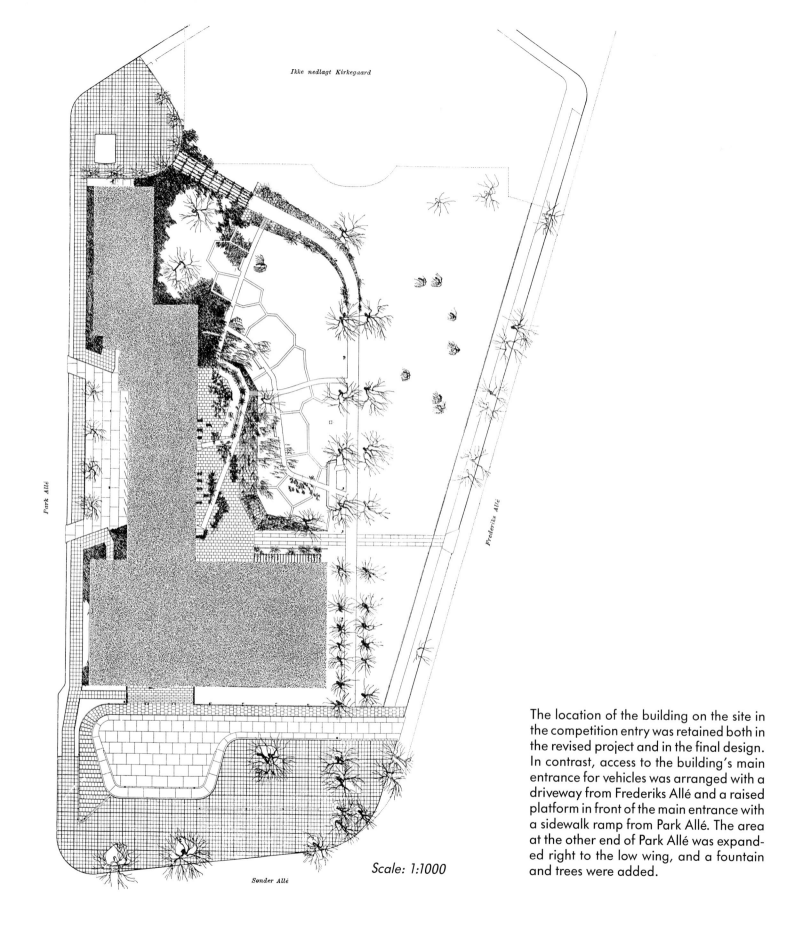

Scale: 1:1000

The location of the building on the site in the competition entry was retained both in the revised project and in the final design. In contrast, access to the building's main entrance for vehicles was arranged with a driveway from Frederiks Allé and a raised platform in front of the main entrance with a sidewalk ramp from Park Allé. The area at the other end of Park Allé was expanded right to the low wing, and a fountain and trees were added.

LAYING THE CORNER STONE AND THE INAUGURATION

Excavation work had progressed so far in the course of the summer of 1938 that the cornerstone was laid on September 25th.

Prime Minister Stauning and Minister of the Interior Dahlgaard were to have laid the first two stones, but were prevented because of the tense situation in Europe. Instead the task was performed by two members of the building committee, Stecker-Christensen and J.C. Sørensen, while Mayor H.P. Christensen laid the last stone.

In spite of the war and occupation, work progressed briskly, and on July 2, 1941, Aarhus was able to celebrate its 500th birthday with the inauguration of the City Hall. Crown Prince Frederik and Crown Princess Ingrid attended the inauguration and conveyed King Christian X's best wishes on the occasion.

Erik Møller's son Jørn raising the flag on the morning of July 2, 1941

Everyone who had worked on the building had gathered in the square in front of the City Hall. And they all cheered when the flag was raised.

Crown Princess Ingrid signing the City Hall's guest book

All of Aarhus had assembled on and across from Rådhuspladsen and the Crown Prince and Crown Princess were obliged to step out onto the balcony to received their adulation.

The City Hall seen from Banegårdspladsen, 1990

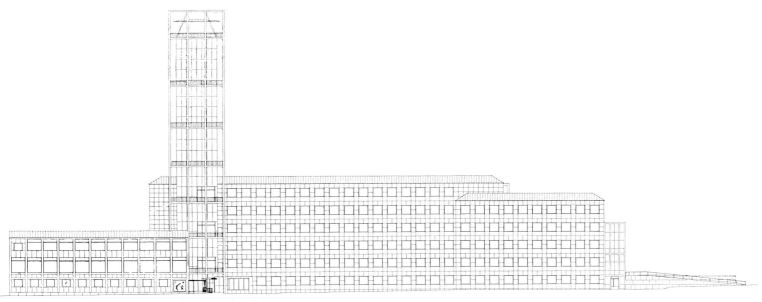

Facade on Park Allé

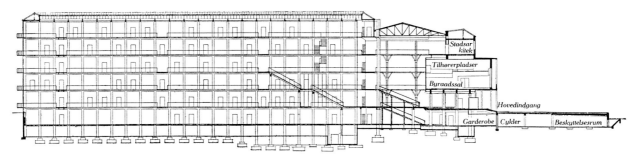

Longitudinal section of the high wing

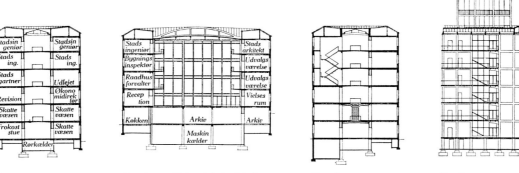

Section *Section of the Main Hall* *Section* *Section on a scale of 1:800*

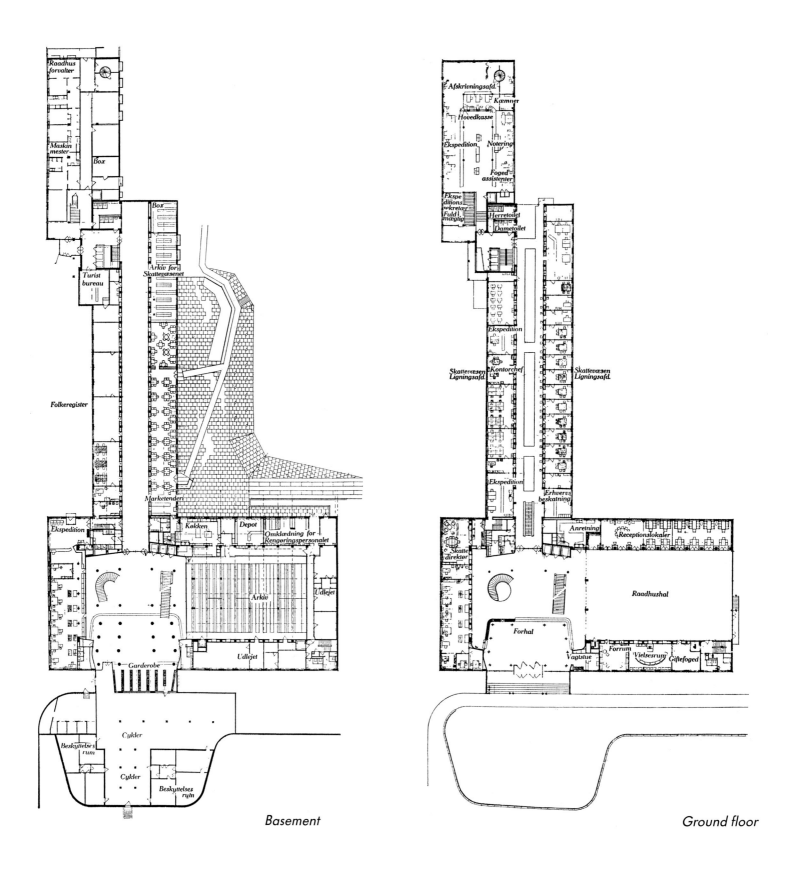

Basement

Ground floor

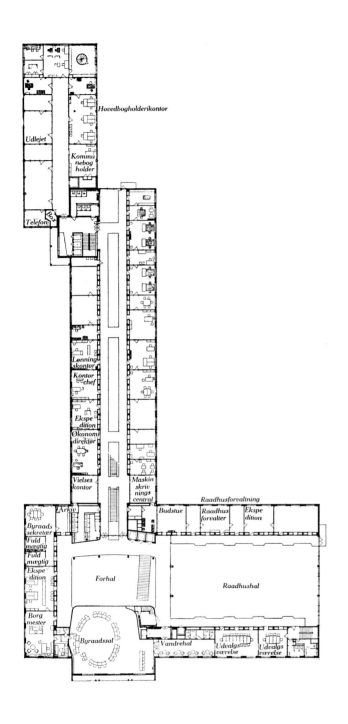
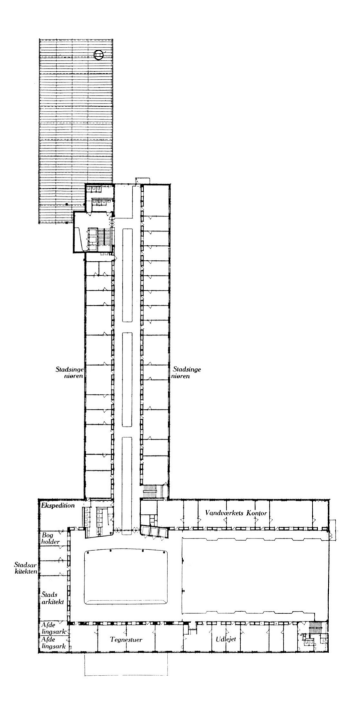

1st floor　　　　　　　　　　　　　　　　2nd floor, on a scale of 1:800

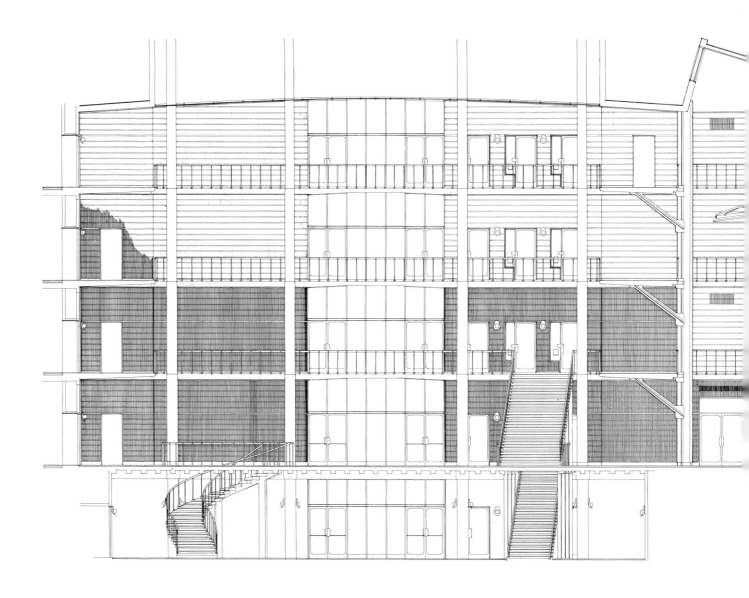

Scale: 1:150

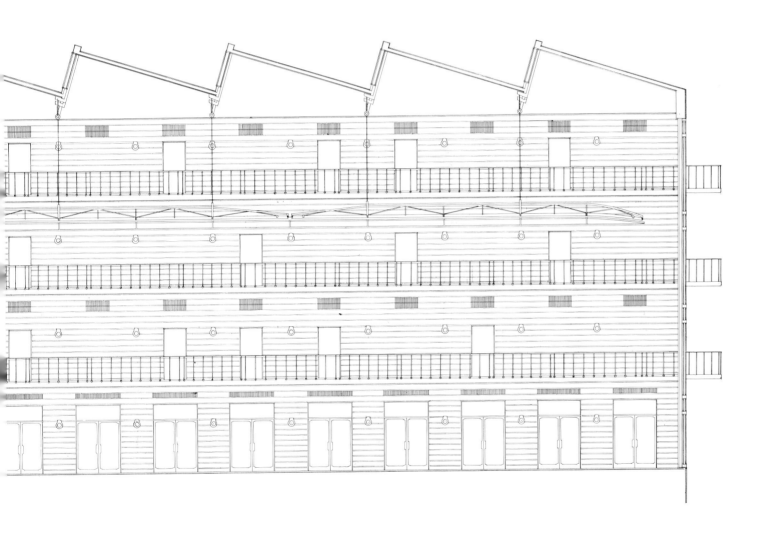

The section shows a screen construction hung under the skylight in the Main Hall. The screen was to have regulated the acoustics of the room, but was luckily eliminated.

Facade mod Frederiks Allé

The City Hall seen from Banegårdspladsen 1990

AARHUS CITY HALL

Constructions, materials, and artistic decoration
by Erik Møller

The City Hall can be termed a "solid-cast reinforced concrete building" since both the outer walls and the floors are bearing structures in their entirety. Only the main walls were made as reinforced concrete skeletons to provide for hot-air ducts, etc. The building is divided into bays measuring 3.15 m, and all crosswalls can be moved without making constructional changes.

The main walls have recesses for each bay which can be fitted with doors from the corridor or with closets from the offices.

The low wing with the tower contains a large office for the public that can be reached from Park Allé. The outside appearance of this wing is different, since the large windows which were deemed desirable to provide light in the fairly deep office led to the use of a reinforced concrete skeleton – something that was also better suited to the construction of the tower.

The building is faced with marble from Porsgrunn, Norway.

The balconies with external columns were cast using white cement and an aggregate of calcined flint. Wooden molds were used for the casting, and the hardened surface was sanded with Carborundum.

The roof is covered with copper. "Perspektiva" windows were used for the offices, with Oregon pine sills and teak frames. The large window sections in the Main Hall and the corridor of the office wing have steel frames.

The building is supplied with district heating from the city utility company, and the offices are heated by radiators placed under the windows and by the injection of hot air whose humidity can be adjusted to prevailing conditions. The corridors and the Main Hall have radiant heat provided by heating coils cast in the balconies and in the floor of the Main Hall. The Main Hall also has a hot-air system which is used

The Main Hall

particularly on special occasions. The walls in the Main Hall are covered with beech slat panels. The building is divided into three intimately linked sections: 1) the hall section, with the Main Hall, the City Council Chamber, and reception rooms; 2) the high office wing, with a large number of offices, and 3) the low wing with the tower, with large offices for the public.

All corridors to the offices in the first two sections were made of corbelled reinforced concrete slabs. The office wing was built as a panoptic corridor with both overhead light and side light. Side light from the high windows on the south gable reaches far down the corridors since the inside balconies only extend all the way to the window on one side.

Sidelight is also very important in the Main Hall, where the large west window opening on the avenue in the old cemetery dominates the room.

The City Council Chamber is supported by 12 columns and placed as a block projecting into part of the vestibule. Strong overhead light strikes the outside of the Chamber's wall, making it a distinctive element in the Main Hall.

Wall and ceiling coverings were chosen to ensure proper acoustics after a model of the room had been subjected to a number of tests by Dr. Vilhelm Jorden under the direction of Professor P.O. Pedersen.

The walls of the office wing are made of blockboard with beech veneer in panels between the visible reinforced concrete pillars. All visible reinforced concrete elements in the Main Hall and corridors are plastered. This is true of the columns and ceilings of the balconies, for example.

The City Hall's surroundings were designed in close cooperation with the municipal authorities. The street areas were designed in collaboration with Messrs. Rambøll and Smith-Hansen, and the park in collaboration with the city gardener, Mr. Sandberg.

The existing trees were preserved as far as possible and constitute the park's main element.

Along the old cemetery avenue, which has been retained as an avenue along the large window in the Main Hall, there is a broad pedestrian path from Rådhuspladsen down to Banegårdspladsen. The avenue-like character gives way in the park to scattered trees, and at Rådhuspladsen the avenue ends in a group of trees creating a framework for Mogens Bøggild's sculpture "The Pig Well."

Johannes Bjerg's fountain "Agnete and the Merman" was erected on Banegårdspladsen, and Svend Rathsack's female figure in the park.

The panoptic corridor, office floors in the high wing

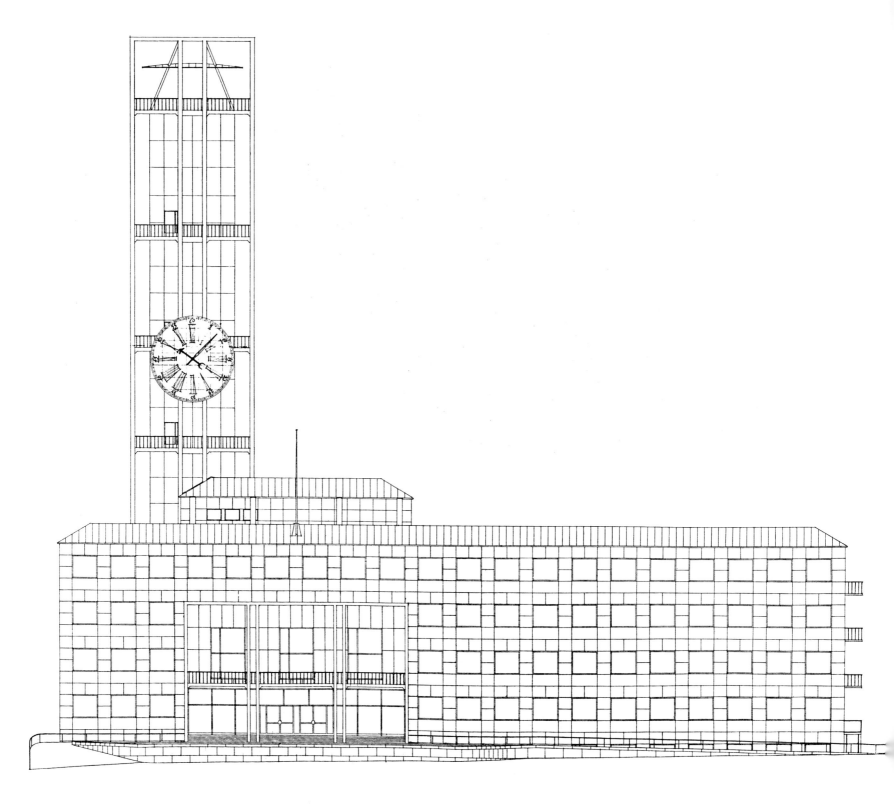

Scale: 1:150

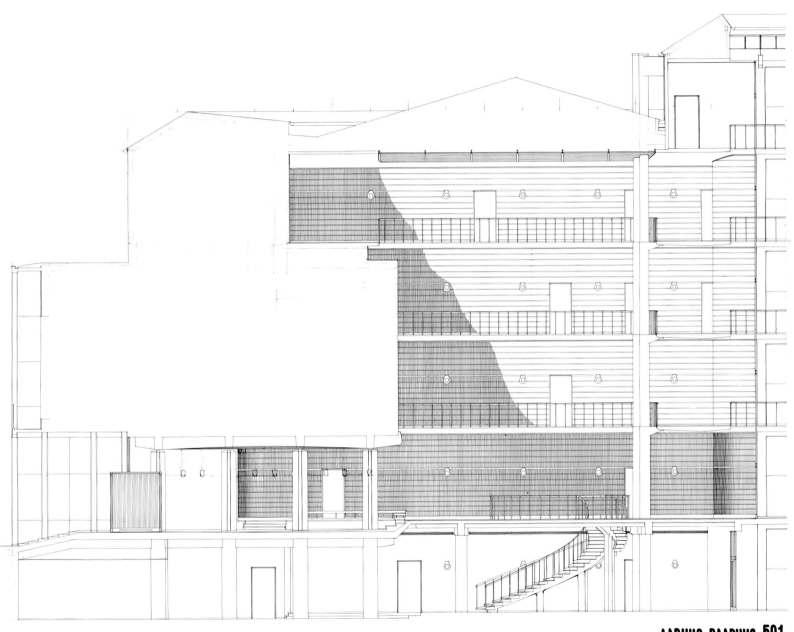

Scale: 1:150

The high wing's gable seen from the park

The gable window in the high wing

Benches in the vestibule

Paneling in the high wing

A sign in the Main Hall

DETAILS

The City Hall was designed down to the smallest detail; even door knobs and keyholes were designed and bids for them requested. This is how things were done then, and today's selection of acceptable fittings did not even exist.

Signs for the City Hall were all made with an alphabet designed for the purpose modeled on the sans serif "Grotesque" type.

A shield-shaped screen creates a backdrop for the speaker on the podium in the Main Hall. A similar screen sets off the Mayor's seat in the City Council Chamber.

ABCDEFG
HIJKLMNØ
PRSTUVXYZÆ
1234567890

AARHUS RAADHUS 1122.
ÆNDRET ALFABET
ARNE JACOBSEN ERIK MÖLLER
ARKITEKTER M.A.A.

The City Hall's alphabet

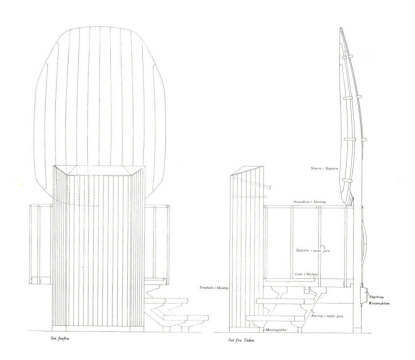
The speaker's podium in the Main Hall

Wall lamps at the entrance

In Aarhus City Hall the architect Hans J. Wegner had his first greater assignment. In collaboration with the architects in-chief he designed interiors, furniture and details. Some similarity can be traced from these early works to the furniture, that made Hans. J. Wegner worldwide famous.

Bids were requested for light fittings and other equipment for the City Hall following designs by the architects.

The light fittings were made of mat-finished brass with a specially shaped glass cover.

Bracket lamps were originally used in the corridors and balconies while pendant lamps were used in offices and larger rooms.

In the course of time, requirements for artificial lighting have changed, in the offices in particular, and new fittings have replaced the original ones.

A bracket lamp in the Main Hall

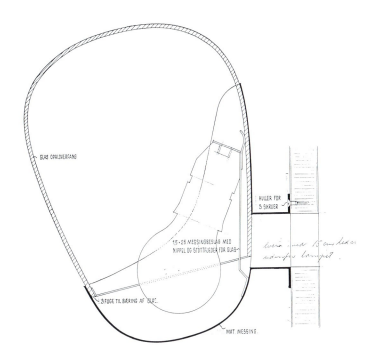

A bracket lamp in the corridors and halls

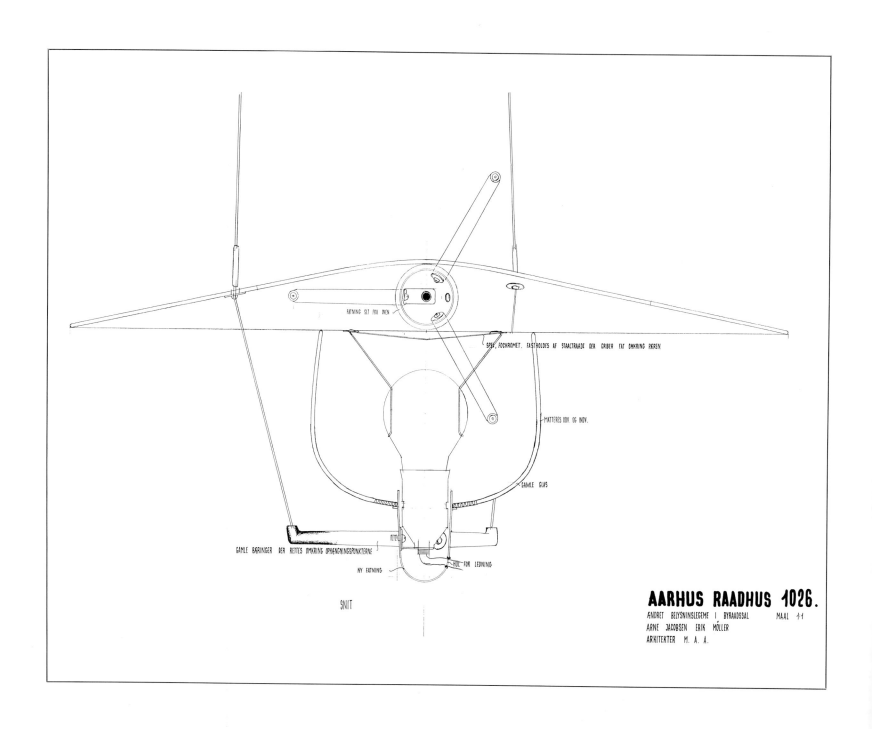

A lamp in the City Council Chamber on a scale of 1:3

A clock in the high wing

A chair in the Civil Wedding Room

A stacking chair in the Main Hall

The back of a chair in the City Council Chamber

A design for a carpet for the Mayor´s office

49

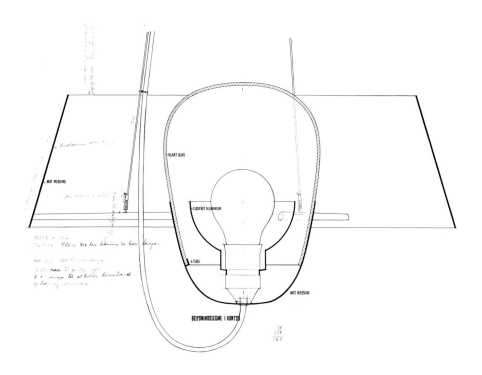

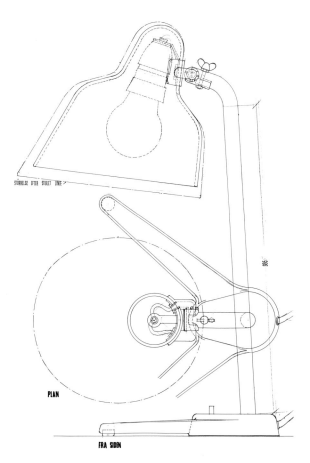

Scale: 1:4
Original drawing
on a scale of 1:1

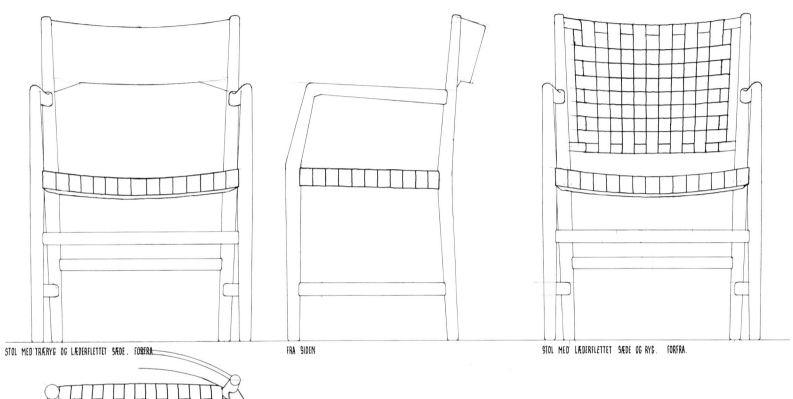

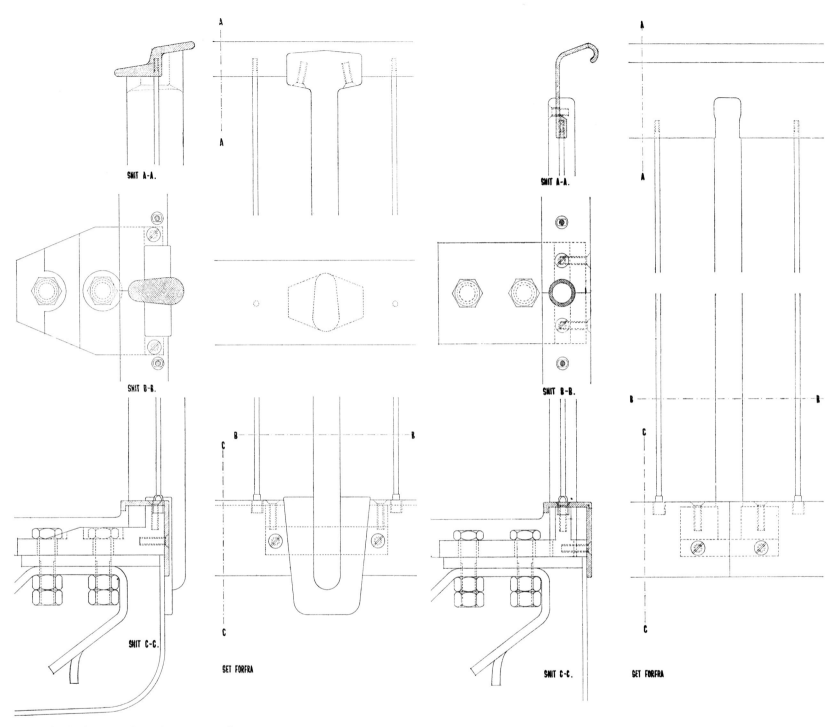

The balcony rails in the Main Hall

The balcony rails in the office wing, on a scale of 1:3

The banisters on the balconies and along the staircases have brass handrails made by Nordisk Kabelfabrik especially for the purpose. The balustrades on the balcony are made of cast iron and are fastened to mounts cast in the reinforced concrete. The balustrades are placed at 40-cm intervals, interspaced at 5-cm intervals with wire. The brass handrails were left untreated and today are beautifully polished. Originally they were to have been patinated a dark bronze with shiny wearing surfaces.

The facade's marble facing

THE MARBLE FACING

Porsgrunn marble, quarried near Lien in southern Norway, was chosen for the building's facing. Obtaining the material entailed a number of problems because of the war.

A/S De Ankerske Marmorbrud quarried the marble, and since it was most economical for the company to have the blocks sawn up in Norway, they were transported by ship to the company's largest quarry in the vicinity of Narvik, in northern Norway, to be sawn into slabs. The first third arrived at Grenå harbor in February 1940 on the "Blåmannen." The ship had to dock at Grenå instead of sailing direct to Aarhus because of difficult ice conditions, and the slabs had to be taken by truck to Aarhus. The ship was icebound for the rest of the winter and later was sunk by a mine. The second third of the c. 6000 cubic meters of facing stone arrived with the "Herfinn," which was attacked from the air during the voyage. The rest of the slabs were obtained by sending blocks by rail from the quarry to Copenhagen, where they were sawn into slabs. The material was then sent by rail to Aarhus. As a result of all these difficulties, it was not possible to complete the facing until a very late stage in the construction work.

THE BOG OAK FLOOR

All of the offices have oak parquet floors, while the floor in the Main Hall is made of bog oak.
Bog oak is definitely a "shortage material" since it can only be obtained by digging up peat bogs on a large scale. The bog oak was the cause of much concern.

Only a very small percentage of the large tree trunks that are pulled out of peat bogs can be used as timber. When the wood is extracted it is waterlogged and must be dried very slowly and carefully to keep it from splitting before it is cut, a process which must be carried out while the blocks

of wood are still wet. Since it was a hard winter, all the wood that had not yet been dried or placed in heated rooms splintered completely in the cold. Occurring just a few months before the inauguration, this problem almost changed all our plans.

The bog oak floor in the Main Hall

THE MAIN HALL

A number of iron ties, 10 cm. thick and 20 m. long, were cast in the sawtooth roof over the Main Hall. Because of the difficulty in obtaining materials, it was impossible to find ties long enough, and the only way to solve the problem was to weld them out of small pieces. The authorities consequently required that the ties be put to a tensile test before they were put in place. The test was carried out in a U-shaped reinforced concrete girder which had to be cast for the purpose. Oil pressure jacks were used to create the necessary tension. The weldings held in the test as we had predicted even though a few of the welded iron pieces started to "float." But when they had stopped, they tolerated the tension that was required of them. For safety's sake these pieces were nonetheless replaced by another type of iron with greater tensile strength.

Tensile testing the iron in the Main Hall's sawtooth roof

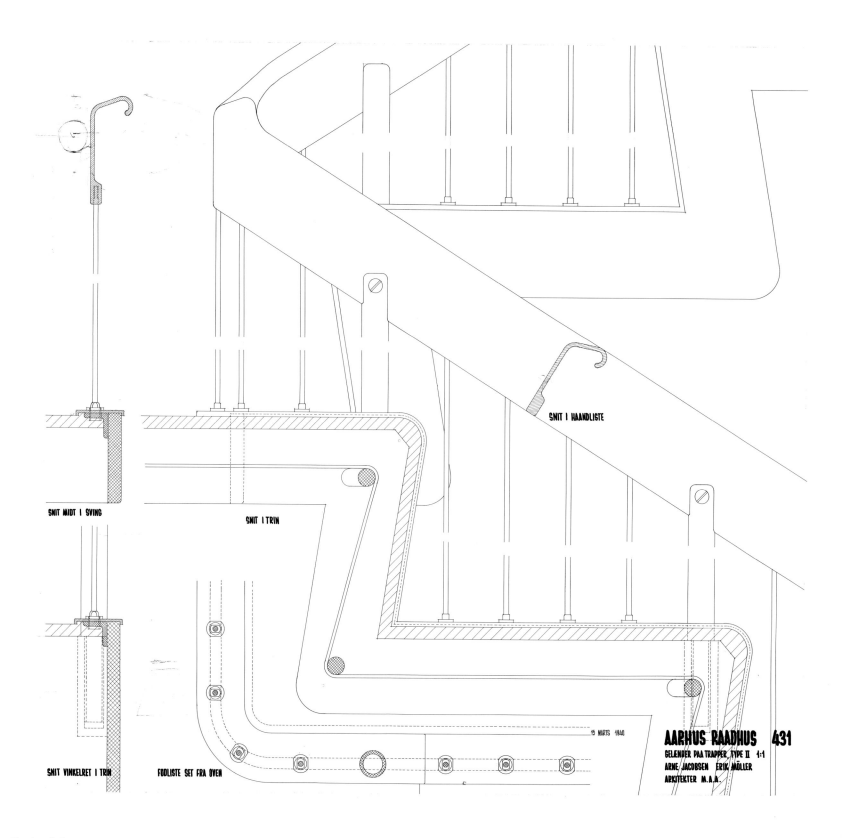

Scale: 1:3

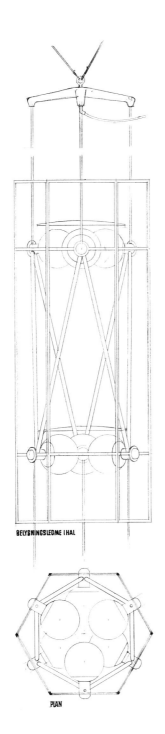

Scale: 1:15, 1:3

THE MAIN HALL

The Ny Carlsberg Foundation financed Hagedorn Olsen's mural in the vestibule.

THE CITY COUNCIL CHAMBER

The walls of the City Council Chamber are faced with Cuban mahogany panels and the floor is covered with a thick pile carpet woven by "Troba" in Sønderborg. The carpet bears a schematic map of Aarhus. The chairs and fronts of the City Council members' tables are covered with pigskin. A number of portraits of former mayors hang on the walls.

THE CIVIL WEDDING ROOM

The painter Albert Naur decorated the Civil Wedding Room. Floral decorations were painted directly on wooden panels. The center wall is decorated with bouquets of summer flowers; the two end walls have spring and autumn flowers. Naur painted the walls from large bouquets which he picked in the municipal flower parks (with the city gardener's special permission) and in the meadows on the outskirts of the city. The autumn wall was begun first, followed by the walls with the other seasons. Naur painted a test bouquet of meadow flowers which I picked in Marselisborg Forest. The furniture in the Civil Wedding Room is painted white and the seats of the chairs have loose cushions covered with a hand-woven green-striped fabric. The carpet was woven especially for the room with motifs taken from nature.

The painter Eiler Krag working in a committee room

THE COMMITTEE ROOMS

Aarhus received a number of presents on its anniversary, including funds to be used to decorate the City Hall. Competitions were held for painters and sculptors for a number of the commissions.

Professor Kræsten Iversen was commissioned to decorate the two committee rooms adjacent to the City Council Chamber. The decoration consists of a series of large landscapes from Jutland: the west coast, the moors, central Jutland, and the east coast.

Eiler Krag was commissioned to decorate a committee room. He painted a frieze with motifs from Aarhus: Clemensbro, market day by the Cathedral, the pier, and Banegårdspladsen. The friezes were painted directly on the plaster with casein.

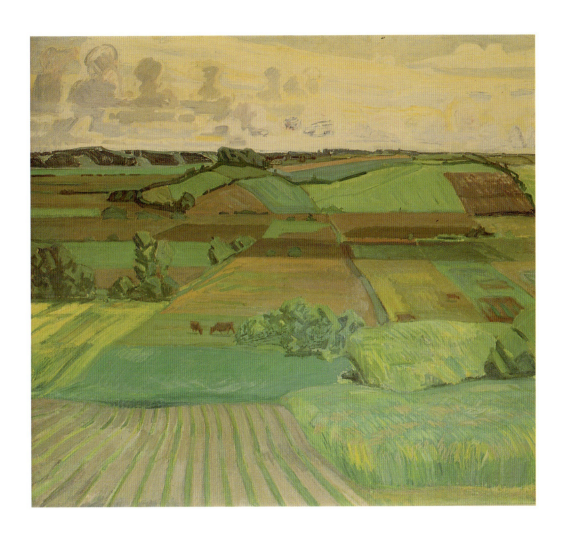

Erik Møller, Kræsten Iversen, and Arne Jacobsen inspecting the competition entries

THE VESTIBULE

The two reliefs in the vestibule were made by the sculptor Anker Hoffmann. One shows fields being sown; the other depicts a number of men struggling with a large block of stone – conceivably one of the seats for the thingsted.
The reliefs are made of "giallo fleuri" limestone.

Mogens Bøggild made the design and cartoon for a mosaic in the vestibule. Because it was feared that the very finely detailed work of art would be unable to stand up to the busy traffic across the vestibule floor, it was decided to place it on a wall instead.

Agnete Varming executed the mosaic; she is seen here working on the project together with her assistants.

AGNETE AND
THE MERMAN

THE PIG WELL

The sculptor Johannes Bjerg's fountain "Agnete and the Merman" was placed in a basin of Porsgrunn marble in front of the gable of the low wing on Banegårdspladsen.

The Ceres Brewery donated the cost of Professor Mogens Bøggild's sculpture "The Pig Well." The composition on Rådhuspladsen on what was formerly Lindeallé was designed in collaboration with the architect Kaare Klint. Bøggild's first design depicted the story of "The Prodigal Son" who returns home and must eat in the pigsty, but this story was eliminated in Kaare Klint's design.

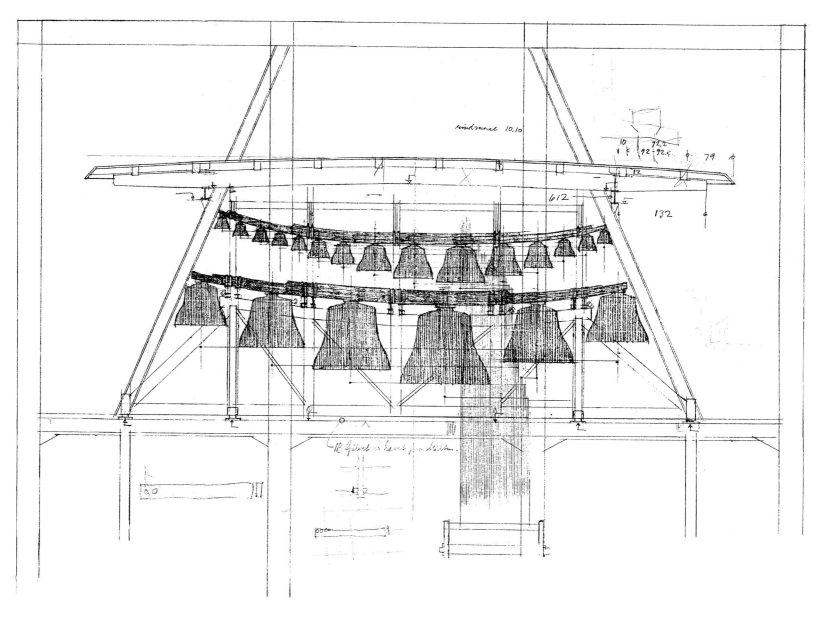

THE CARILLON

The shortage of metal during the war made it necessary to launch a campaign to collect copper and tin to cast bells for the City Hall tower. The campaign was a great success, bringing in nearly 10 tons of metal. The organist of the Church of the Savior in Copenhagen's Christianshavn quarter, Mr. Rung-Keller, served as our advisor and composed the carillon melody, taken from Morten Børup's "May Song" from c. 1500.

Quarter past the hour

Half past the hour

Three quarters past the hour

Striking the hour

The panoptic corridor seen from the upper floor of the vestibule

THE DRAPED STRUCTURE

by Kjeld Vindum

"It is the architect's task to create rooms which are warm and good to live in. He therefore decides to place a carpet on the floor and to hang four coverings which create the four walls. But one cannot build a house of fabric. Both the carpet on the floor and the coverings on the walls require a constructive structure in order to hold them in place. Creating this structure is the architect's second task" (Adolf Loos in "Das Prinzip der Bekleidung," 1898).[1]

The addition of the tower is probably the most conspicuous of the changes which the prize-winning entry for the competition for Aarhus City Hall underwent in the process of reaching its final form.
An equally interesting change was the covering and rounding off of the more sober and austere winning entry that were also a result of this process. The use of coverings and rounded edges represents a softening of early Modernism, but it was also an essential element in the special development of modern Nordic architecture in the years prior to the second World War.

Composition
The City Hall is built up as a modern composition consisting of four primary building elements – the half wing, the high wing, the low wing, and the tower – which cut into one another. In addition there are

three secondary elements: the City Council Chamber, which projects from the main facade over the main entrance like an independent element; the ramp, with the basement level under the main entrance; and the tourist office, which projects from the corner between the tower and the high wing. This type of organization for large buildings, as an asymmetrical composition made up of rectangular boxes, each clearly defined in itself, is typical of modern architecture. The boxes are most often linked at right angles, forming T or L shapes. Walter Gropius' Bauhaus Dessau from 1926 is one of the best known early examples. Links between boxes placed in the same direction, but staggered, are also frequently found. A well-known example is Hannes Meyer's school in Bernau from 1828–30, which was the model for Aarhus University's similarly staggered design. Both types of link are represented in the composition created by Aarhus City Hall's three large wings.

The staggered link between the high and the low wings was found in the competition entry, where both wings were organized with central corridors, designed in such a way that the western zone of offices in the low wing was a direct extension of the high wing's corresponding eastern zone. This special, clear, and elegant link was, as pointed out by Jørgen Sestoft,[2] introduced in Denmark (if not discovered) by Vilhelm Lauritzen. He used it in the competition entry for a municipal school in 1928, on the one hand, and in the Danish Broadcasting Corporation's building, on the other, the latter published in project form for the first time in 1934. The same trick was used by Kay Fisker, Povl Stegman, and C.F. Møller in the first buildings for Aarhus University, which was completed in 1933.
In Aarhus City Hall, however, the central corridor in the middle story of the low

A column in the vestibule under the City Council Chamber

wing was replaced by a large continuous room in the final design.

The building elements thus cut into and overlap one another, but except where the City Council Chamber protrudes through the office zone towards Rådhuspladsen and into the vestibule itself, the office zones serve as buffers so that the overlappings do not interfere with the regularity of the inner rooms. The plan is built up on a grid with 315-cm modules, expanded to 349.5 cm in the low wing. The backbone of the otherwise asymmetrical design is the main axis, which extends from the main entrance through the high wing. The entrance section, City Council Chamber, vestibule, and high wing are largely symmetrical around this axis, while the Main Hall is symmetrical around a transverse axis.

Otherwise the vestibule as a type – a covered atrium with overhead light and balconies along the walls[3] – has forerunners in both National Romantic city halls such as Nyrop's in Copenhagen (1892–1905) and Östberg's in Stockholm (1911–23) and in Neo-classicist buildings such as Edvard Thomsen's and G. B. Hagen's Øregård Senior Secondary School (1923–24), its arched glass ceiling very like the ceiling in the vestibule of Aarhus City Hall. The type is also found in Gunnar Asplund's various designs for an addition to Gothenburg City Hall, from the Neo-classicist competition entry from 1925 to the final design.

The primary volumes in Aarhus City Hall are arranged with great sensitivity and attention to the site's special conditions. On the one hand, the building takes up a relatively small amount of the plot in comparison with most of the other competition entries. On the other, it makes an elegant division of the remaining areas into a square and a park.

On Parkallé, the building blends in with the densely built urban milieu, while towards the west it opens up on the more spacious and greener area with fewer buildings. In those days there was an army barracks; today there is the Concert Hall with a park laid out in front of it.

Soft contours

In comparison with the competition entry's very clear, terse plan, the final plan is freer, more rounded, and in general characterized by softer contours. This move away from the sharp-edged regularity of early Modernism represents a trend which was nonetheless already visible in the competition entry: for example in the freely curved entrance ramp, in the oblique, rounded-off design of the City Council Chamber, and in the oblique divisions between the halls, which cling around the staircase, placed off center. This softer line was first suggested in the work of Gunnar Asplund, the mentor of Jacobsen and Møller, in the Bredenberg department store in Stockholm (1933–35), among other things in the beautifully rounded "durchsicht" and in the cloakroom screen in the canteen. And naturally the most common reference, Asplund's remodeling of and additions to Gothenburg City Hall (1934–37), also has several free-formed curves, first and foremost in the furnishings, but also in the way the two new meeting halls are separated from the Main Hall. These trends towards a softer line are also found in Sven Markelius's Bygnadsföreningshus in Stockholm (1934–37) and are fully developed in his Swedish pavilion for the New York World's Fair in 1939, where all the typical characteristics are found.

They were equally pronounced, however, in Lauritzen's winning entry for the competition for Kastrup airport three years earlier. It had rounded contours, oblique angles and the irregularity they create, free curves, zig-zag contours, and other features.

Alvar Aalto introduced rounded contours on a smaller scale in the plan for his sanatorium in Paimio (1929–1933), where we already find freely curved contours in the roof over the main entrance. And in his library in Viipuri (1930–35), the vestibule at the back entrance is designed as a symmetrically curved form – not unlike the design for the ramp in the competition entry for Aarhus City Hall.

But as Stuart Wrede writes, "the limp curves of Asplund's courtroom walls and judges' desks at Gothenburg are in marked contrast to the dynamic forms Aalto employed in the Viipuri library and the Finnish Pavilion in the 1939 New York World's Fair. The influences in this area that may have flowed back and forth at this time between the two arhcitects remain to be explored in detail."[4] What Wrede does not note is that the rounded contours and soft curves are also manifested in contemporary projects designed by Jacobsen (with Møller as his collaborator). Examples are Bellevue (1933) and Stelling House (1934). And they were used more extensively than in Asplund's work. (As they were in Palle Suenson's work for Privatbanken from this period.)

In any event, a special softening of the plan took place in Scandinavia in the middle of the 1930s. It was a trend which in Denmark probably culminated, as Sestoft noted,[5] in Lauritzen's airport, but one which Jacobsen was largely instrumental in defining. In this development in particular, Asplund's role was less important. And even if Aalto was the one who sowed the seed, his curves developed in a completely different direction.

In the plan for Aarhus City Hall, these features are found concentrated primarily around the vestibule. Examples include the way in which the office zones of the high wing cut into the vestibule, with ob-

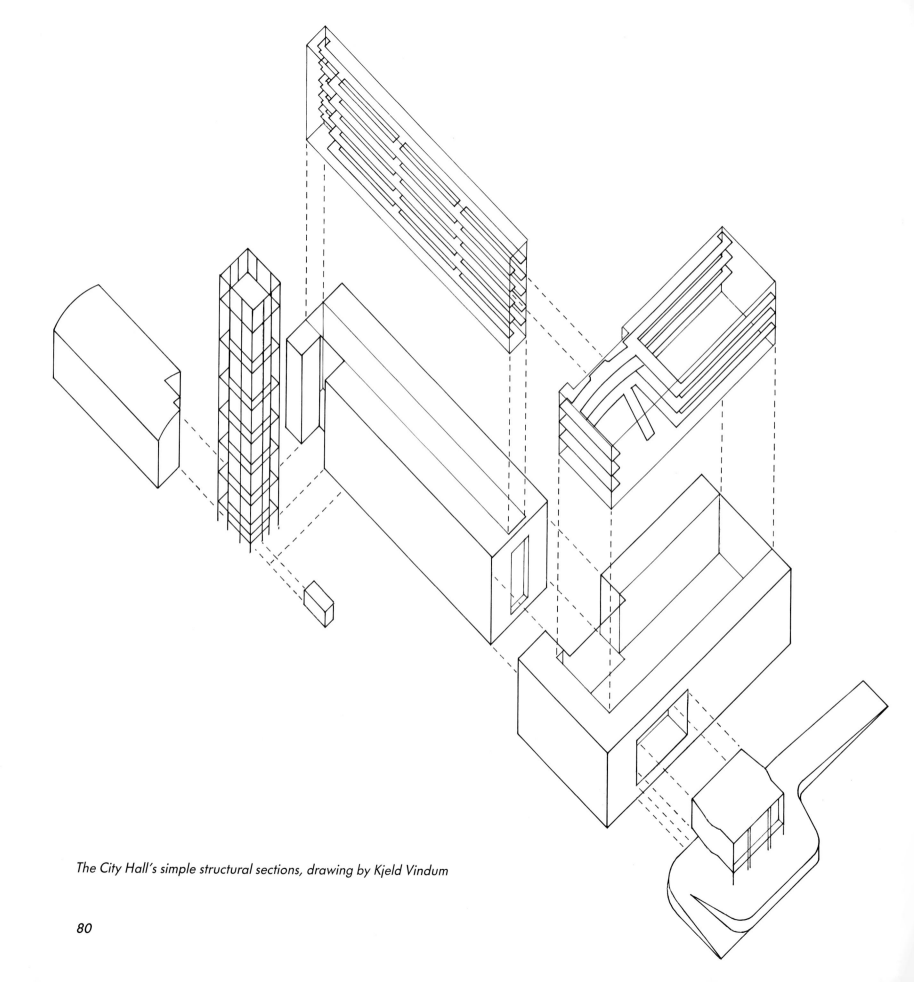

The City Hall's simple structural sections, drawing by Kjeld Vindum

lique, rounded contours symmetrical around the longitudinal axis; the rounded contours of the City Council Chamber in the vestibule (which are highly reminiscent of the contours of the meeting halls in Gothenburg City Hall mentioned above); and the reflection of this contour below in the demarcation of the entrance areas from the floor in the vestibule. Other examples are the staircase to the first floor, which is placed off center in the room, and finally the winding staircase to the basement. Another important element is the entrance ramp, whose design diverges markedly from that in the competition entry but is still rounded. The basic form is now a trapezoid. The rounded trapezoid, also found in the contour of the City Council Chamber, was one element used by Lauritzen in his airport design.

Rounded contours
There are far more rounded contours in the interior than those that directly result from the plan.
For example, the concrete bearing structures are rounded throughout with a smooth plaster. This is perhaps most conspicuous in the vestibule, where the visitor moves among the rounded, cross-shaped columns that support the rounded and slightly arched reinforced concrete grid, which in turn supports the City Council Chamber. Elsewhere in the building circular or H-shaped columns are used.
Rounded, cross-shaped columns are found for example in Mies van der Rohe's pavilion in Barcelona (1929) and in his Haus Tugenhat (1928–30). But while Mies's columns – like Le Corbusier's round ones – have the same thickness throughout and meet the floor and ceiling without any intermediary element, the columns in Aarhus City Hall are slightly curved on a vertical plane, are rounded at the top, and are liberated from the construction they support almost to the core. In order to emphasize their independence from the construction as a whole, the top of each column is fitted with a brass cap, while the transition to the floor is mediated via a brass strip.

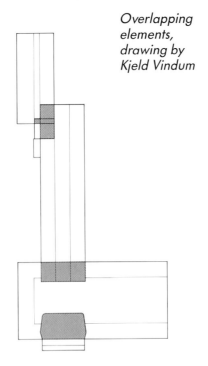

Overlapping elements, drawing by Kjeld Vindum

The modern column and the classical are thus fused in such a way that it is impossible to say that one dominates the other. (In his much later and stylistically more classical building, the National Gallery in Berlin (1962–67), Mies incidentally used cross-shaped columns which are also cut off at the top and liberated from the ceiling construction they support almost to the core of the column.)
The same trend, to liberate constructive elements – the bearing and the borne – from one another is also expressed in the transition between the concrete grid and the actual mass of the City Council Chamber. This transition in particular is not plastered up in a cavetto or rounded. On the contrary, a clear differentiation is made between the two elements. This effect is emphasized by having the grid continue past the demarcation of the City Council Chamber and pulled over the edge as if to get a better grip on the mass it supports.
The tendency to keep elements free of one another is also manifested in the two places where the balconies meet the transverse glass partitions. The balconies as it were give way to the vertical element in a rounded recession. The same thing happens when the balconies meet the large windows and continue on the outside of the building. The balconies in the Main Hall, in contrast, widen at regular intervals in a similarly rounded contour.

Softened edges are also found in most of the building's doors that are fitted with glass. The edges of the glass panels in both metal and wooden doors are cut at a flat angle. (Is this a simplification of the Rococo's pilaster strips?) This feature is incidentally also found in Aarhus University's earliest building.
The interior has several examples of rounded contours, culminating in the City Council Chamber, where practically nothing is sharp or squared off.

Beveling
The two main wings, which are otherwise the most regular and sharp-angled elements, have rounded, or more correctly beveled, contours. Low copper-covered roofing is namely inserted as a "mediatory" slanted surface to soften the transition from the vertical wall to the actual roof. In reality, the roofs are divided into several slightly slanting or curved surfaces which end at the outside in the roof that we see. And by extending the outer walls with a battlement one could easily, as in most modern houses, have achieved the effect of a flat, or rather invisible, roof.
If the gutter is seen as a substitute for the classical cornice, then the slanted roof surface can be seen as a minimalization of and a reference to traditional roof forms. But the roof form used here is also found in classical architecture, among other things in the Thorvaldsen Museum in Copenhagen and the old City Hall in Gothenburg. And when Asplund used the same roof form for his addition to Gothenburg City Hall, it was an expression of a desire to have it harmonize with the old City Hall. Naturally the low, mediatory roof also emphasizes the fact that the City Hall actu-

A section of the facade seen from Frederiks Allé

ally does not have a flat roof. The very earliest modern buildings had already revealed the problem of using flat roofs in northern climes, and there was thus every possible reason to experiment with other forms. On the City Hall's low wing, where there is no overhead light, a slightly arched roof was used of the type known from factory buildings, for example B & W's Rosenkjær hall in Copenhagen: a simple and genuine modern roof form which was a product of the industrial age's use of steel and concrete rafters.

In the competition entry, however, the same roof had been used on the low wing as on the other two wings. The arched roof was added to the design at the same time as the tower.

The tower

The tower is built around a core containing stairs, elevators, and landings. The tower's closed core is 9 m. wide, 7 m. deep and 54 m. high, and, like the rest of the building, is covered with marble slabs. "Scaffolding" is placed around the core. This concrete construction, which supports the six balconies and two clocks, brings the tower's total height to 60 m. The distance between the three lowermost balconies corresponds to two stories, or nearly 8 m., while the distance between the three uppermost gradually increases to over 10 m. Atop the viewing platform, the construction supports a light roof over the carillon. The first designs for the tower show a thicker version with identical vertical divisions and with the clocks placed uppermost on the broad sides. Both the location of the clocks and the vertical divisions were, according to Erik Møller, inspired by historical towers in Pisa, Verona, and Assisi. Initially the architects had wanted a tower separate from the building, like a campanile. But features in contemporary Italian architecture may also have influenced the design of the tower.

Guiseppe Terragni sketched a tower (never executed) for the Casa del Fascio in Como (1928–36) which, like the City Hall's tower, has a lattice construction, but with bells located on the second highest "sto-

ry." There is no less resemblance to Ignazio Gardella's competition entry for a tower for the Piazza del Duomo in Milan (1934), where a staircase fixed between two plates, in the same way as the core of the City Hall tower, is surrounded by a lattice construction. But like the first two sketches for the City Hall tower, these projects lack the differentiations in the horizontal division which so markedly contribute to the elegance of the completed tower.

Beveling is found here, too, namely on all the lower inside corners of the construction.

As a direct result of the tower's construction, the protruding City Council Chamber and the low wing have skeleton constructions, with the skeleton exposed in the facades. In the low wing this change was also due to a decision to replace the original division of the middle story into smaller offices around a central corridor by a large continuous room which required larger windows.

The exposed skeleton construction was a well-known feature in Italian rationalist architecture, but Asplund also made use of it in Gothenburg, where it is found in the facade of the addition to the City Hall, as an element in its harmonization with the old City Hall's facade. The skeleton construction here emphasizes the division into bays and differentiates the facade in depth, as the cornices and pilasters of the classical neighboring facade do. In Aarhus City Hall, the main entrance, with the protruding City Council Chamber, was also changed and given a skeleton construction. In the competition entry, the City Council Chamber's projection was only supported by two columns. Now the City Council Chamber is in a way framed by a skeleton construction so that two pairs of columns divide up the whole entrance into three. As a whole, there is a link with the classical type of city hall, for example C.F. Hansen's City Hall and Court House in Copenhagen (1805–15), with its temple-like main entrance, even though the entrance to Aarhus City Hall is placed asymmetrically in the facade.

Facing materials

In the competition entry, the outer walls of the City Hall were described as plastered with light cement. The windows, like the gutters, were to be painted white. All this was changed.

The facades were originally to be more open, appearing as skeleton constructions, filled out with windows surmounting light-weight panels of a darker color. In the final building, the openings are smaller and the horizontal and vertical ribs in the skeleton consequently broader. In addition, the panels under the windows have been incorporated into the wall. The whole building is covered with slabs of Norwegian Porsgrunn marble divided in such a way as to retain the original skeleton construction look in the sense that the areas that correspond to the ribs of the skeleton are covered with almost square slabs of equal size, while the areas that correspond to the panels under the windows are covered with slightly recessed double-sized slabs. (Another difference is that the surface of the lower panels was sandblasted while the other slabs were rolled with steel balls.)[6] Otherwise no major changes were made to the two large wings. Balconies were, however, added outside in continuation of those inside the large windows. Except for this, the

Overhead light in the panoptic corridor

gable of the Main Hall, with the large window section and its beautifully proportioned segmentation, for example, was only changed slightly. The design of this gable in particular creates an eminent interplay with the trees outside. Both of these window sections have steel frames, while the others are made with sills painted white and varnished teak frames. The marble facing was almost demanded by the public, and it in any case satisfied two of the needs that were expressed in the many protests over the original project. It added dignity, if not monumentality, to the building and it linked it with the great tradition of monumental architecture. In addition, it did not arouse the same horror of nakedness which was largely evoked by early Modernism.

In the late 1930s, facing in general became more widespread in modern architecture, first and foremost in buildings of a more monumental character.
Jacobsen's Stelling House was covered with ceramic tiles, as was Lauritzen's building for the Danish Broadcasting Corporation, while Asplund's Skogskirkogård Chapel (1935–40) was covered with stone. The use of stone for facing became very widespread, perhaps especially in Italy. One of the most obvious examples for comparison here is Gio Ponti's first office building for Montecatini in Milan from 1936, which also has large, smooth, marble-faced facades with uniform, regularly placed windows.

Covered interiors
With the exception of the wall in front of the City Council Chamber – which forms the background for Hagedorn Olsen's controversial mural – the walls in the vestibule and Main Hall are covered throughout with beech slat panels. In the high panoptic wing, all the walls – the panels filling out the visible reinforced concrete skeleton – are covered with beech veneer on blockboard. Finally, the City Council Chamber is lined with panels of Cuban mahogany. The use of paneling was justified among other things by its positive

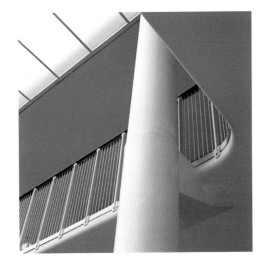

acoustic characteristics, but here, too, it is an expression of the trend towards the classical.
The City Hall's architects had been brought up with Neo-classicicm, which was both the start of Modernism and the object for its rebellion. Neo-classicism marked the beginning of the purification of overfilled, draped interiors demanded by Modernism. But covered interiors also survived in Neo-classicism, for example in the differentiation between various types of rooms. And it is precisely this period's treatment of walls, with either simple panelling or painted surfaces, to which the City Hall's interior first and foremost harkens back. For example, it is not very far from the atmosphere of the smoothly panelled police chief's office at Copenhagen's Police Headquarters to that of the City Council Chamber at Aarhus City Hall. In Erik Møller's and Flemming Lassen's library in Nyborg (1935–40), the whole interior open to the public was covered with smooth, veneered blockboard. The same was true of Asplund's Gothenburg City Hall addition.
As a whole, wood-faced interiors gained ground during this period, something that cannot just be attributed to a trend towards the classical, but must also be seen as an expression of a trend towards a rapprochement with nature, letting the interior assimilate the surroundings outside. It was a trend which was not just manifested in the increasing use of unpainted wood, both in the form of panels and in the use of interior constructions, but also in the use of unplastered walls of brick or stone in interiors.

In the City Hall, wood is the material used first and foremost. For example, the marble floor that was planned for the Main Hall was replaced by bog oak parquet. All the furnishings and nearly all the furniture are made of varnished wood. Except for ordinary office chairs, which have seats of plaited calfskin, pigskin seats are used. All the handrails and such fittings as door handles, ashtrays, bracket lamps, etc. are made of brass. All the materials are kept in a warm, golden color scale and have an exquisite finish which invites one to touch them. They have a special tactility with an unmistakable sensuality, a feature of the period's reformulation of modern architecture, especially in Scandinavia, but one which was applied with special elegance and generosity in the City Hall. The rounded contours and wall coverings seem to culminate in the front of the building, actually in the very first room, the City Council Chamber, and then recede gradually back towards the tower and the low wing. The tower does not even have any wood visible. The walls are plastered smooth and painted white, and the elevator shaft is built up of glass and white-enameled steel. Even the beveling of the door frames mentioned previously was left out of the elevator doors, the only place in the building where this was done.

The draped structure
One of the central themes used in Aarhus City Hall, as noted above, is modern architecture's assimilation of aspects from the classical tradition.
In this respect, there may be reason to view the building in relation to the widespread trend which prevailed throughout most of Europe in the years prior to the Second World War.
"In the 1930s, parallel with a rethinking in the figurative arts, there emerged in

The panoptic corridor in the high wing

Europe a common architectural language that transcended ideologies and political régimes and in which two factors – realism and tradition – were always present, though in varying degrees." This is how the Italian historian of architecture Franco Borsi characterizes what he calls the monumental era.(7)

The World Exposition in 1937 was proof that tradition and monumentality were in the air again. Of the many buildings, Le Corbusier's Pavillon de l'Esprit Nouveau was the one least affected by this trend. Modernism's abrupt break with tradition and history had caused quite a hangover. And monumentality was needed for public buildings, especially in totalitarian Germany, Italy, and the Soviet Union.

Monumentality and links with history are also what people in Aarhus demanded when they were presented with the winning entry for their new City Hall.(8) But as in Scandinavia in general, "the monumental era" was expressed here in a special and very subdued way which largely rejected the use of monumental clichés and whose traditional features were of a more subtle and less heroic character.

An opening towards the tactile, the use of uncovered natural materials, and the revolt against early Modernism's sharp-angled regularity were indeed elements in the monumental era's architecture. But they were also manifested in the Modernism which did not bow to traditionalism and monumentality. So even though Le Corbusier, for example, was relatively untouched by this trend, "his own postwar work shows a significant change in direction. The most striking evidence of this is the change from crystalline forms and precise detailing derived from the use of smooth rendered surfaces and steel and glass curtain walls, from which all suggestion of material substance has been abstracted, to the use of massive sculptural forms, tactile surfaces, and crude detailing associated with the use of raw concrete, brick, and wood. Although the immediate cause of this change was no doubt the shortage of steel in the postwar

period in Europe, it also seems to have been the result of a change in attitude that was already manifest in his work in the 1930s."(9)

In the City Hall, this development was probably expressed as a merging of trends which, however, are manifested here in a completely different way. The change over from crystalline forms does not result in massive sculptural forms but in softening and beveling, in a cultivation of soft contours. Detailing does not promote crudity: on the contrary, it is extremely delicate, and tactility is not rough but rather smooth and refined in its differentiation.

All in all, we can say that Aarhus City Hall probably reflects the trends of its day in the development of modern architecture, but that it does so in a very special way. The most important reason for this is probably that there was never a complete break with the classical tradition in Scandinavia. The attitudes from what Demetri Porphyrios has called Scandinavian Doricism and Doric sensitivity(10) largely lived on in modern architecture. Scandinavian Doricism refers to the special, simple, artless classicism whose links with traditional architecture were intact and with which the whole generation of early Danish modernists, among them Jacobsen and Møller, was raised.

Elements of this powerful tradition, which had been present the whole time as an undercurrent in early Danish Modernism, were found in the late 1930s in what was later called the functional tradition. Among the earliest and best-known expressions of this trend is Aarhus University and Flemming Lassen's and Erik Møller's library.

In Aarhus City Hall, both classical features and a clear feeling for tactility, for material effects, can be seen as an expression of this tendency.

But while the functional tradition primarily points back to specific aspects of Doricism, the simple and artless effects, and the more rustic tactility, the interior of the City Hall in particular has a sophistication found in its details and surfaces and an elegance in its lines which have more to do with the special sensitivity associated with Doricism.

Even what is considered one of the most important examples of Danish Doricism, Copenhagen's Police Headquarters, outwardly more somber and heavy, shows a move in the direction of refinement which, like its fine finishing and slightly elitist look, invites comparisons to the City Hall.

"There is not, either in the conception or its working out, a single hint of vulgar or commonplace thought. There is, on the contrary, a fine feeling for refinement in the expression of civic character which has been imparted to all those sections of the building to which the public normally has access. And, in addition, the building has humanity in detail, for there is gaiety... and there is evidence of subtle enjoyment... There is freshness in this detail work." This is what the English architecture critic, Howard Robertson, wrote about Copenhagen's Police Headquarters in 1927.(11)

The same thing could have been written about Aarhus City Hall. Both buildings exhibit the contrast which Markelius noted in Sigurd Lewerentz's Resurrection Chapel in Enskede from 1923. Here he contrasts "pure language of form, clarity, logic, and taut monumentality – with the transi-

The staircase from the basement to the vestibule

tory stylistic detail – seductive elegance."(12)

The origins of this interest in detail, in elegant lines, in smooth surfaces, and in luxurious materials, including the use of brass together with dark woods, can naturally be attributed to the Empire style. It, too, "veiled the geometrically shaped rooms and covered walls with artistic draperies which ... at times were gathered up at the ceiling to resemble a tent."(13)

The City Hall's links with tradition can first and foremost be found here: in the end of Neo-classicism that combines Doric simplicity with the Empire's cultivation of detail, of the elegant and the luxurious, and in its softening of geometric sharpness.

But the City Hall, like Asplund's later work(14), also contains features which can be interpreted as Gothic.

This is true, for example, of the conception of space in the vestibule and the panoptic corridor, both of which open upwards towards the heavens. But it is also true of constructional features such as the slightly arched ribbed structure under the City Council Chamber which at a single point is borne by cross-shaped columns. Like the H-shaped columns, they may bring to mind the clustered columns of the Gothic.

No matter what the mutual significance of the many sources of inspiration, tradition and the formal expression of international trends in Scandinavia constitute a special niche in the modern architectonic room, a niche which, in addition to the architects responsible for the City Hall, was defined by such important figures as Asplund, Markelius, and Lauritzen. It is a niche whose special formal characteristics are a soft contour inside a regular volume, the line formed by draping a precise structure in a room.

Nordic mist
Copenhagen's Police Headquarters represents Neo-classicism on its way towards Modernism. The same can be

said of the work of Vilhelm Hammershøi, who painted his last picture in 1915, five years before Police Headquarters was finished.

Hammershøi's famous interiors bear many similarities to Aarhus City Hall as far as composition is concerned: rectangles which press up against or cut into one another around displaced axes in an interplay of right angles broken by curved lines added by people and furniture.

These compositions also show a kinship with aspects of more tradition-bound Cubism, represented for example in Vilhelm Lundstrøm's painting "Architecture" from 1932, where the division of the surface by straight lines around a clear axiality is played out against a series of curved lines. Two elements which, however, clearly differentiate Hammershøi from Lundstrøm are color and light.

In addition to black, Hammershøi's palette is dominated by gray, brownish, and yellowish tones, corresponding to the City Hall's stone, mosaics, wood, and golden brass. It is precisely in relation to this color scale that Hagedorn Olsen's powerful "Modernistic" colors – especially his dominating blue – create problems. Subdued colors which, together with the soft light – generally that found in overcast weather – and the resulting sensitive modulation of tones are what give the contours in Hammershøi's pictures their characteristic softness.(15)

It is characteristics like these which have led the painter Per Kirkeby(16) and the Norwegian architect Sverre Fehn(17) to speak of "the Nordic mist" which dissolves solid shapes and veils constructions. This mist is a symbol of the Nordic vision in contrast to the clear, sharp vision of the Mediterranean countries.

Against this background, early "white" Modernism's interplay, with sharp edges and strong colors, served as a hole in the cloud cover which let the harsh Mediterranean light through, casting its reflections on the North.

Aarhus City Hall shows that the mist settled once more, but the melancholy which often follows the mist, and which, for example, fills Hammershøi's pictures, never managed to settle on the City Hall.

Powerful features such as the elegance of its lines and surfaces and their special sensuality resisted.

Aarhus City Hall is one of the Danish buildings from this century which is most often mentioned in the international literature on architecture.

This is probably because the softening and the rounded contours of Modernism found in the City Hall are an expression of an especially Danish or Nordic attitude.

The building reconciles modernity with the traditional, with nature, with the monumental. It is an obliging, generous, and sensual building which brilliantly avoids all that is populist, banal, and vulgar.

It is a highly complex but also very rich building that will stand as a monument in the Danish architecture of this century.

Many other things and much more could be said about it than was said here.

Notes:

1) Adolf Loos: "Das Prinzip der Bekleidung," in "Ins Leere Gesprochen, 1897–1900," Vienna, 1921, p. 139.

2) Jørgen Sestoft: "Arne Jacobsen og det nordiske" in "Arkitekten Arne Jacobsen 1902–71," exhibition catalogue, School of Architecture, Aarhus, 1990, p. 49.

3) Kenneth Frampton: "Modern Architecture, 1920–1945," New York, 1983, p. 276. This type is described here as fundamentally Doricist, with reference to Scandinavian Doricism mentioned later.

4) Stuart Wrede: "The Architecture of Erik Gunnar Asplund," Cambridge, Mass./London, 1980, p. 171.

5) Jørgen Sestoft: op. cit.; p. 52. Lauritzen's airport is mentioned here as a possible source of inspiration for the plan of Aarhus City Hall.

6) According to Erik Møller, bits of metal chips from this treatment are the reason why the lower slabs have a slightly warmer tone.

7) Franco Borsi: "The Monumental Era," New York, 1987, p. 52.

8) See: Kjeld Vindum: "Aarhus Raadhus" in SKALA, No. 11, 1987, p. 18.

9) Alan Colquhoun: "The Significance of Le Corbusier" in "Modernity and the Classical Tradition," Cambridge, Mass./London, 1989, p. 175.

10) Demetri Porphyrios: "Scandinavian Doricism" in Architectural Design, No. 5/5, 1982, p. 22.

11) Howard Robertson: "The Police Headquarters at Copenhagen" in The Architect & Building News, February 18, 1927. Quoted after a reprint in Howard Robertson and F.R. Yerbury: "Travels in Modern Architecture," London, 1989, p. 31.

12) Stuart Knight: "Swedish Modern Classicism in Context" in International Architect, No. 8, 1982, p. 14.

13) Hugh Honour: "Nyklassicismen," Copenhagen, 1979, p. 152.

14) Stuart Knight: op. cit., p. 14.

15) See: Poul Vad: "Hammershøi," Copenhagen, 1988.

16) Per Kirkeby: "Naturens blyant," Copenhagen, 1978, pp. 84–86.

17) Mathilde Petri: Interview with Sverre Fehn in SKALA, No. 23, 1990, p. 12.